Griffon

Books by Stephen Dobyns

Griffon

Poems by Stephen Dobyns

New York *1976* Atheneum

PS
3554
.02
G7
1976

Acknowledgements are due to the editors of the following publications for permission to reprint poems in this book.

AMERICAN REVIEW: *Our Place in Winter, Looking for Spring.*
ANTAEUS: *Death of a Small Businessman; Learning to Talk; Seeing Off a Friend.*
BIRD EFFORT: *Absence, Covetousness; Crossroads; Griffon; November; Spider.*
KAYAK: *Boredom; Despair; Escaping Again; Getting Around Town; Gluttony; Greed; The Lives of the Chosen; Moving Through Spain; Patience; Shoes; Sloth; The Television Poems; Ten Guests for Dinner and Conversation; Today There Was No Mail and No Phone Calls.*
LILLABULERO: *Getting Through to the End; Having My Teeth Cleaned.*
THE NATION: *Dancing.*
THE NEW YORKER: *Envy; The Grandfather Poem; Grief; Spite; Silence.*
NEW LETTERS: *Hands; Putting It All Away.*
NORTH AMERICAN REVIEW: *Changing My Mind; Ivan Shark Addresses Me Briefly (under the title "Being Talked to"); Late Afternoon; Running.*
PEQUOD: *Anger; Bravado; Doubt; Fear.*
POETRY: *Clouds; Play in Four Acts; Six Poems on Moving; Six Poems on Not Moving; The Survival Variation.*
POETRY NORTHWEST: *Getting Away From It All.*
SENECA REVIEW: *The Men with Long Faces.*

Thanks are also due to the National Endowment of the Arts for a fellowship, and to the Corporation of Yaddo and MacDowell Colony where a number of these poems were written.

Library of Congress Cataloging in Publication Data:
Dobyns, Stephen, 1941-
Griffon: poems.

I Title.
PS3554.02G7   811/.5/4   76-10213
ISBN 0-689-10736-6

For Mekeel

Contents

PART THREE

PART FOUR

PART FIVE *GRIMOIRE*

Part One

Griffon

Distrust men, hate horses—
they mock me with four legs.
They cannot fly. Men hunt me
to make cups from my talons,
bows from my ribs. Hear me laugh.
Such things will not bring them luck.
The one-eyed hunt for the gold
I draw from the mountains.
Horses carry it. Men fight over it.
I find it. You with one eye,
trespasser, protect yourself.
You feel the wind behind you.
I am that wind. You join me,
then leave me, tumbling into the clouds.
Try thinking they will catch you.
They will let you down.
Name me. I am earth and sky.
I am protector and delver.
You think me a creature
of your dreams. You are mistaken.
You are the creatures of mine.
Name me. I am Griffon.

Hands

for Liza

Refusing love, work and nourishment, my hands
   lie before me: pale tubers, skinned rabbits,
   surrounded by pencils and papers.
My hands will not touch them.
The day is too much with them.

They are like plants pulled from the soil, curled
   and drying at the edge of the garden.
They are like tourists who, having learned
   of cholera in Italy, return to their London hotel
   and take the next flight home.

I tell them they are lucky and let them compare themselves
   to the dry hands of undertakers, the thin hands
   of accountants, the moist hands of the poor.
I show them the long fingers and small palms
   of politicians: crippled jellyfish, five-legged spiders.

I explain that the palm is a rose, that the fingers
   are roots questing for soil.

I explain that the palm is a bed
   shared by a husband and his four thin wives.

I explain that the Big Dipper is the hand of a beggar,
   that Cassiopeia is a pair of hands offering water
   to the thirsty.

I give them definitions: All hands on deck:
   A Swedish massage. Promiscuity: A free handout.
   Burlesque: A show of hands.

I warn them about the world: Two hands
  went into an alley; one came out.
  There was soup for dinner.

I tell them that the hands of poets are small and pink
  like the curled ears of retired boxers.
They beleaguer the bare breasts of their women.
They can be seen on the street, rising from baby carriages
  like pink clouds before the beaming faces
  of their nurses.
They can be seen slipping into basement cafes
  to sip herb tea which they stir with their fingers.
They can be seen lying in the display cases of bakeries,
  sugar-dusted and wrapped in poems about their vacation,
  their first child, their thirtieth birthday.
A seashell is the atrophied hand of a poet.
A pigeon's beak is the poet enraged.
A jelly doughnut is the poet who has stopped writing
  and returned to business.

By the time I am done, it is dark and the moon has risen
  and there are nighthawks over the street.
My hands lie quietly.
Tomorrow is still a promise of blue sky:
  a day of friends when hands are for soothing
  in a world pushed back to newspaper distance.
I will tell my hands how well they look, how young,
  and they will again believe in themselves, take
  nourishment, give love, begin any work and succeed.

Putting It All Away

The wind from the mountains is closing my doors;
it is time to begin forgetting.

    I'm sitting in a chair with a woman
    who is reading me a story.
    The story is green. It sounds
    like wind or morning light.
    I am the story she is reading.
    The woman smells of babies.
    I put them aside.

I begin forgetting like changing my clothes.
I have gone to a funeral: black shoes, black suit.
They smell of dust; I lock them away.

    I am in a hospital. There are nails
    in my leg. I shout into a rubber cup.
    I hang from the edge of a star, then drop.
    Two goats and the smell of vanilla fall with me.
    In the morning there is cream of wheat
    and a boy with freckles and stories of escape.
    I put them aside.

As I begin forgetting, I grow thinner.
Sadness is five pounds, pleasure three.
When I am done, I will be light or air:
something to see by, the draft that shuts the door.

    I stand by a bonfire. Chickens
    without heads run circles around me.
    Above me the body of a deer hangs
    upside down. Its stomach is slit open.

I see my friends and family waving,
calling from the belly of the deer.
I put them aside.

When I am done forgetting, I will forget
my name, and priests will come and give me
a new one. Or perhaps I will have no name,
and when I am told what has been done
or not done, or when police come or men
with brittle prizes, I will say he just left,
never arrived, doesn't even ring a bell.

I am in the kitchen. Something is baking.
I take dry mittens from the radiator.
The mittens are warm. There is the smell
of fresh bread, shaving soap in the morning.
A man and woman embrace in the center of the kitchen.
The whole house is like red mittens.
I put them aside.

Escaping Again

Rising, I leave my body sleeping
on the brass bed. For all your pleasure
you could be a machine. I touch the walls.
I touch all the hands in my house.
My clocks fold into little cubes.
I touch myself all over: those arms and legs,
that expanse of white and dying skin.
I am leaving to join the companions of winter,
turn air to ice and study the death of fire.
The rest of you can stay in bed.
I shall become a student of fur and lie down
among the wolves. I shall catch elk with my teeth
and grow like winter wheat beneath the snow.
Far to the south my body is sleeping: idler
with its breakable dreams. There is no
temperature in that room. All your blood
is sitting down. I have come back for you:
you who are embarrassed by the nakedness of trees.
Hear me and my brothers singing. We are
dancing in the street: four paws and pointed ears
against the moon. Don't look for help.
Your neighbors are surrounded by a blue light.
They sit on their hands and accept stories from machines.
They can do nothing. All their clocks are dying.
Free you, find you: you don't even know
you are lost. We have returned to your place
of four walls: I and the moon and the death of fire.
We see you at the window with your hands
and negative face. No glass can save you.
Break it, find yourself another zoo, you
stupid son-of-a-bitch, come down out of that house
and run. We are all creatures of a dead moon.

Today There Was No Mail And No Phone Calls

The mailmen and telephone operators
are calling it a day. For hours
they have been banging their bare bodies
among mailsacks and disconnected wires.
They call it love, but I have received no messages.
Beneath the bags and piles of clothing
are notes to me reading:
Beware the woman in the red dress;
The truck that will smash yours
is crossing Pennsylvania; You will die
tomorrow, or, conversely, You are loved.
At the other end of disconnected wires
someone wants to ask the question
that will send me to Florida and good fortune;
someone wants to tell me not to leave the house.
I wouldn't think of leaving the house.
My safety is in the hands of strangers
who are right now pulling on their clothes
and thanking each other for the good times.
They are the wall between all my warnings.
I climb into the evening without eyes.
I enter tomorrow like a blind man
walking to the edge of the sea.
The tide is always coming in.

The Men With Long Faces

The men with long faces have come after my knives.
They put their ladders against the sides of my house.
They put their heads through my windows, all pressed together
like the spines of old books. There is much law within them.
My knives are taken and packed carefully in cotton.
How shall I be known from my animals without them?
How shall I keep apart the corners of my rooms?
The men with long faces speak of new futures and welcomings.
They ask my response, promising comfortable houses.
I grease my hands and the men try to shake them.
My knives fill with laughter like firemen at field-days.
How shall I now read the night without them?
How shall I know which stars are lying?
They are carrying my knives to their wagons of boredom.
The street lights come on and each one is singing.
Their music is empty. It breaks on the pavement.
The men with long faces are driving their wagons.
Their wheels turn over to the sound of the singing.
Tied down in the back, my knives are forgetting.
How shall I know what is quiet without them?
How shall the darkness now keep its distance?

Changing My Mind

Discontent is the roof of the house
in which I live. Each wall is boredom.
Each floor is indifference. This is the place
I am leaving. From my attic window,
I watch two poems fight it out
with knives in the front yard. Darkness
rises from them. I built this house
and all its entertainment. Now I am going.
Builders crawl toward me on white bellies.
What would I do with your new walls?
All my poems are fighting in the street.
They do not see me as I sneak down
the back stairs and out the door. The smell
of freshly cut grass sweeps over me. The sun
wraps me in color. I run down the road
like a thin dog chasing a red truck.
I won't come back.

Running

The sky is what I see
of the hand of which the sky
is the center.

The hand on the sheet
is beginning to close.
The sheet closes up within it.
I am in a far place,
getting farther.

Two stones—I make a wall.
Two stones across from it,
another wall. A line of stones
beneath me. Now I am running.

The hand above me
is beginning to close.
Fingers draw up the horizon.
Silence is the wind within the hand.
Which winter is this one?

One to hide from;
one to take with me. The wall
falls behind me as my fingers
press into it.
Love, speak to me quickly.

A finger touches my voice.
My voice is gone. It touches
my hands. They are gone.
Feet grey, getting greyer:
dark place I am running through.

The sheet becomes part of the hand
as you begin to recede. Be
careful, Love. Where am I
coming from when I leave you behind?

The sky closes. The sun
breaks apart. Falling over me
it becomes the ashes
of the place I have run through.
What chance to say goodbye?

Learning To Talk

I introduced you to my words
and sent them traveling. The nouns
went north to a winter they had always
been expecting. Verbs kept on running.
Adjectives dawdled. The others, the smaller ones,
sought out suitable retirement. They opened
gift shops in Phoenix, scoured Europe
with cameras. They learned to play golf.
I have found a new language
where the words live together.
They line up in neat rows like creatures
waiting for the sun. I am waiting with them.
I am sitting in the room's dark surrounded
by your face—Arabs from the south
tell of suns like that one,
journeys like this one.
Now I begin my first story.

Ten Guests For Dinner And Conversation

They arrive by car from the other side
of the street light. They wear the same face,
maybe John Wayne's face. It doesn't matter.
Hello, John. They say they are starving.
We hurry to the table, so hungry that we
ignore the knives and forks and use our hands.
Roast dictionary, newspaper soufflé, fried poems.
No one speaks. We, good grief, stuff ourselves,
then rub our stomachs, maybe the same stomach.
We can hardly move. Stumbling away, we strip
and climb down into the conversation pit.
Gently, we ease our fingers into each others' mouths.
Slowly, we begin to throw up, then faster,
vomiting over John Wayne faces, Stetson hats.
It gets between our toes which we wiggle;
sticks to our hands which we wave
in an ecstacy of conversation. Talk?
Good god, never before have we said so much.

Getting Through To The End

We have been brought here,
through the name on the wall
we have finally read,
past the man in the burning chair
who has spoken at last.
We have earned this.
We have seen through the eyes of the blind.
We have listened to the music of the deaf.
We have been brought here.
I have companions who I do not know.
They have faces that I cannot see.
I am equally faceless and nameless to them.
We have earned this.
We have come to a dark house.
There are no windows or doors.
We may not go inside.
We have been brought here.
We are allowed to circle the house.
We are allowed to guess at its meaning.
We can talk and touch the cold brick.
We have earned this.
We will stay here, not understanding.
We will begin to grow into the earth.
We will accept the silence of brick.
We have been brought here.
When at last you too come before us,
and stand running your hands over us,
we will be the first of your questions.
You have earned this.

Six Poems On Not Moving

for E.S.

TREE

I copy the clam's silence. My feet
grow into the earth. Across my shoulders,
sparrows discuss their short journeys
and bad neighbors. The sun moves west.
My gaze stalks it to the horizon.

DOOR

I open but never enter. I travel
but never far. Beyond me the room
is thick with discovery. Corners hold promises
past all imagining. Do I believe them?
I swing quietly on my hinges.

FIELD GATE

There is cement in both buckets. I keep
one foot in each. Soon the snow will melt
flooding the field. There will be
a lake. It is still snowing.
I am singing the song that makes it snow.

WIND

The woods whiten; the snow muffles
each tree. I rest among the branches.
Forest of wolves, forest of thieves: they cry
to each other over the broken branches. Carefully
I separate my voice into silence.

REFLECTION

Move and it will break. Touch it
and it is broken. I enter
my future like slipping into water.
The promised reflection shatters.
The life I am living is no longer mine.

PATH

Always running, never moving, I refuse
to be accountable. A place leads its own life:
Whose story are you following? I keep the woods
tight around me. I remain the trace of something
that walked here a long time ago.

Part Two

Our Place In Winter, Looking For Spring

It is March. I am in Binghamton,
New York. As equals on friendly footing, the deer
are moving to the tops of hills to meet spring.
I follow, borne down by northern consequences,
being human. We tilt with the season, keeping
the ambiguities of winter. Like a rich uncle,
spring chooses to meet us. We cannot seek it out.
We wait, then take our chance and follow.

On the mall at the college in Binghamton,
I watch a German shepherd standing by itself.
One paw is planted on a dollar bill. A student
comes and tucks the bill in the dog's collar.
He walks off, the dog follows and everything tilts.
The dog might buy a new collar. It might
meet spring. It could tumble. It could build
a small shack and sell knick-knacks to tourists.

Later, in New Hampshire, I hear spring in the trees
all around me. I can almost touch it, filling the air
pushing around me. I stand on five feet of snow.
I do not choose to sink. I am battered by blue sky.
Sinking is not my decision. The next day it rains
and I decide to leave. The clouds are eating
the mountains. I force myself to believe
that they will be back, that I will come back.

The tilting continues and back in Detroit
the sky is a poor memory of color, perhaps
blue. We point our buildings at the sky
and cock them. They went off a long time ago.
The sky is not falling, we are falling toward the sky.

It won't play catch. Carefully, we put boards
over spring and great signs saying it's about
to be torn down. Only drunks will sleep there.

Very late in a blind pig, I guide a woman,
a lady, who wishes to see such things.
A man wants to fight to get me out of the way—
all for the love of the lady. He would need volumes
of explanation. Instead, my knife is hidden in my hand.
Leaving to avoid trouble, we see the art museum
half a block away. We walk back to our cars over glass.
Those fragments are the flowers of this city.

Today a friend writes to see how badly I reviewed his book.
"I remain more grateful," he says, "that you would accept
the assignment than puzzled by your decision as to how
to treat the poems . . . there's nothing I can do about it,
after all." I think of an egg without its shell,
momentarily together in its own skin. Don't breathe.
I put out my hand, palm forward. Without another hand,
it means stop. There will be spring without us.

Getting Away From It All

I am tired of this complicated life: people
with too many fists and faces like wet stones.
My body will be carefully packed and shipped
to a warehouse in Topeka. Goodbye, long fingers.
May you send word of the ceremonies of rats,
their long lists of essential names.
I shall assume the form of chairs, squat
gracefully in the lobbies of old hotels,
surrounded by bankers with papers and cigars.
Women will sit in me unknowingly.
Interested in rooms, I shall become them.
Interested in machines, I shall take their shape.
I am that car you drive down a dirt road
late at night. I may not get you there;
I could also be the road. I am that mirror
you are looking into and which may not
return your reflection. Suddenly, you look into
the face of a stranger. The door closes behind you.
Or perhaps I will be a kindlier place; a place
where sparrows live in comfort and dogs tell stories
of the winter before last. People too will be admitted.
But I am tired of manufactured things.
I will climb into the mountains
and become a place the water moves through:
a small valley, a mound of stones;
a place where the sky is still a question
and all the trees have tumbling names.
I shall learn the songs of water
and the long green songs of trees and grass.
Closing my hands and eyes, I may learn to sleep there.
Sinking into the earth, I may learn to stay there.

Shoes

I have put aside people like old shoes,
my shoes. Ten pair litter the floor all around me.
They have carried me in dark places
or moments as friends have.
They still litter the floor all around me.
It is almost as if I never had worn them.
The shoes are the strangers. I take
no responsibility for them. If they were gloves
or clothes it would be no better.
If they were as priceless as lions
or cities, golden coins or clear sky,
I would still put them aside,
able to wear them or touch them,
put them on to take them off again.
Constantly changing, I envy them
and wish to be like them, vastly secure
in laces and buckles, or wish
to stand naked on stones without them.
I think of water merging with water,
color with color to become
a huge unimaginable blue.
Instead, I have built a small kingdom:
stone set upon stone.

Moving Through Spain

Spain is a country of small rooms. They
lack windows. They smell of urine. Their walls
are covered with the history of insects,
traces of quick deaths. Between spotted laundry
and the whistle of swallows' wings, courtyards
rise toward a sky of contemptuous blue.

The streets are cluttered with people in transit.
In their left hands are the keys to the rooms
they have come from. In their right hands are the keys
to the rooms promised them. Such rooms are golden.
They have no walls. Pictures hang from the sky,
showing landscapes descending to vast Indian seas.

In Barcelona, on the Calle de Montada, two
thirteenth-century palaces form the Picasso Museum.
No policemen go inside. White walls, velvet walls,
walls of grey stone covered with pictures as clear
as sunlight. International visitors compare pictures
to hometowns. People move as if in church.

A friend says she prefers the palace. Her error
surrounds her. Despite the walls, there are no walls.
A landscape of sleep pushed into a sleepless world.
Only milkmen knock on early morning doors here.
There is no Guardia. I watch the rain spattering
in the courtyard, slipping drop by drop through the ivy.

Swallows swoop and flutter batlike overhead,
whistling in pursuit of the invisible. In Madrid,
three days ago, I watched as pair after pair
of American fighter jets screamed for thirty minutes

over the Prado, more graceful than the best of swallows,
sweeping low in perfect formation over the Prado.

Ducking and clutching their keys, people sheltered
in small rooms and refused to leave. The jets shrieked
with the sound of canvas tearing. In tiny cockpits,
young Americans with faces as smooth as polished stone
played easily with intricate controls. A veteran
of some war told how they flew to keep Spain free.

I would paint them, given the skill, trace their
smooth paths, their little flags, I, who can't even
walk a straight line. My feet speak of writing
and why I came here. If words were nails, I'd
tack down shadows and build a house open to the sky.
Now they are fat and puffy, useless as artillery.

Too many doors open inward here, like the doors
of a theater during a fire. People read papers
to see what day it is. "He feeds them and everybody's
happy," someone tells me. They breathe through small holes
over their mouths. They see through small holes
over their eyes. We approve of it; we pay for it.

Here in Picasso's house the doors open to each other
like flowers: a whole country of red poppies and the small
nameless blue flowers with a yellow star in their centers.
These pictures show pictures no tourist sees. He carries
all color in his eyes; hands swim within his eyes;
words erupt from the corners of his eyes.

The rain continues, but the visitors, having seen
their quota, begin to leave. The rooms darken
to the jangling of their keys. Outside, a troop of soldiers
files past, their boots echoing among the stones,
their rifles shouldered and pointed at the sky.
Clouds move over the city. Swallows wheel and dive.

Late Afternoon

Against the February sky,
the hills, snow covered, rise
one past the other toward the north.
Pale blue is the color of cold.
From the back porch, I watch
something climb the last hill,
moving right to left, man or beast,
a black spot against the snow.
I imagine it someone recently dead.
The sky is a blue cup. Those I
love are far away. Those I would touch
lead orderly lives in rooms to the south.

Clouds

The clouds moved in another hundred feet
during the night, just as they have done
each night for the past two weeks.
Now they hang barely beyond the range
of thrown stones. The sun is someone else's story,
the rich relation of a slight acquaintance.

Bending over us, the clouds have the texture
of faces seen through smoke.
Thoughts in a confused mind look like that.
Tell me again that they are not hostile,
that they have come merely out of curiosity
to see again if we are possible.

If so, then why are doors more difficult to open
as if some sadness were leaning against them?
Why do windows darken and trees bend
when there is no wind? You call that occasional
roar the roar of a plane and I imagine
a time when I might have believed that.

But now the darkness has been going on
for too long, and I have accustomed myself
to the pleasure of thinking that soon
there will be no reason to hold on in this place
where rocks are like water and it's so difficult
to find something solid to hold on to.

November

The rain comes down; my love is far away.
The wind hunts out an entrance to my house.
The grey of autumn trees, leaves blown
to the edges of the street: these are the dead,
clothed in regret. The lowering sky
becomes their winding sheet. My love is far away.
The rain comes down. I watch the river rise.
A yellow rowboat swirls against the flood,
passing south between banks of autumn.
What are the memories of the dead?
I am wrapped in weather, swathed in sky.
The rain comes down; my love is far away.

The Grandfather Poem

John E. Johnston, 1878–1968

I

He is something he is falling into:
a body bunched around him like loose sheets,
old clothes too big for him. His eyes teeter
in their sockets. Bones keep the skin apart.
His face slips toward the mouth and would
slip through it if the jaw weren't locked.
He looks around the room like an animal
preparing to leap. There's no place to go.

The room's on fire. He points to a poinsettia
in red foil. Again he says: the room's on fire.
The horses must be gotten out of the barn.
There are no horses. There is barely a barn.
The years build up behind his eyes.
There is no present. Each person becomes a crowd.
I am a crowd. I see him searching through it
like a child at a fair. I call but he can't hear.

This is a dead house. Pictures of the dead
cover the walls. The roof is rotten. The porch
is caving in. Those who have died sit in chairs,
rest on sofas. In his own room, my grandfather
hunts for the present. I shelter in another,
reading family histories, stories of people
who die quietly in books, in a written silence
where I personally can turn the page.

January in Port Leyden, New York, and
I am here to watch a dying man. His hands
turn back and forth like stranded fish.
At his logging camps, French Canadian
lumberjacks called him the White Eagle.

I remember watching lumberjacks play tag
with bears in the Adirondack forest.
My grandfather's eyes keep sweeping the room.

The obvious questions have been answered.
Pallbearers have been discussed. I am to be one,
other grandsons also. The weight of winter has been
commented upon and the strange behavior of cousins.
Now I am leaving. I take my grandfather's hand.
He holds it, refuses to release it. Startled,
I look and almost fall. His present surrounds him.
Everything topples toward his eyes.

2

A week later, driving north again with my brother
from Michigan through Canada to the funeral,
we drive to the very heart of winter. Arriving,
we are met by my grandfather's nurse at the back door.
She tells me to see my grandfather immediately.
The body is in the front room. She says he looks
so much better than he did last week. This is true.
He lies there like the poor memory of a healthy man.

Children run laps around the coffin, small
cousins, second cousins, some woman not seen
since her marriage in '39. This could be
a celebration or a sacrifice. Give praise
to the man who has gotten through.
We do not see him. We are still running.
Taking our neighbors' hands, we circle the coffin.
There is nothing in the center. This room is empty.

I want to shout: Let this be no surprise but
there is a dead body in this room, hidden beneath
rouge and powder, framed by that amazing
red silk hanging. Pinch him and he doesn't feel it.
Kick him and he shows true charity.
Lumberjacks come into the room, quietly and alone.
They are old and smell of whiskey. They look once
and leave, refusing to sign any book.

It would have been better, cousin, not to be
drunk today or at least not to be holding
that corner of the coffin on these icy steps
which have borne so many. Cousin, be careful
or else our grandfather will give Port Leyden
a memorable goodbye when the box slips and twists
down the long hill to the center of town. Cousin,
will you put him back when he has made his resurrection?

We never buried him or saw him into the ground,
which refuses to accept the dead in winter.
We left him in the basement of the cemetery chapel
in what looked like a wine rack but held coffins instead.
Nine were there already, and the undertaker's assistant
swore that one had been opened. Just slide it in
and leave it. A wave of the hand and slam the steel door,
still echoing on what was never a funeral.

The Arrival

Grey flecked paint, splashes of
orange for the rust, steel panel upon
steel panel rising above the wheat.
A dark blue funnel with a red stripe,
black smoke drifting back over the
upper deck and cranes into the fog.
There is no sound from the turbines.
The bow cuts through the field, trees
brush against it as it passes.
Across the hull, "America" is printed
in huge letters. I see my grandfather
on the bridge. He waves to me.

Part Three

First Meeting Ivan Shark

Casually, as if in passing, I meet
Ivan Shark and his daughter Fury.
He tells me he is Death and I laugh
because he is only on its side.
His face darkens. Words roll out
from the corners of the room; they
roll toward him, into his mouth.
I am Death, he says again, and again
I laugh. Anger covers him like a wind.
The furniture moves toward him,
rolls toward him, into his body.
We face each other in the empty room.
I am Death, he says a third time.
Now the walls lean toward him;
the floor tilts and I start to fall.
Suddenly we are standing on a flat place
by a river. I laugh again:
Each of Death's instruments
think they are Death itself. You
are only my death, a mere beginner.

The Ivan Shark Alternatives

Ivan Shark is being very funny, as is
Fury, his quiet daughter. I'm not laughing.
Ivan Shark is holding his sides with his
fat fingers; his mouth's open and I can see down
to the pits and stench of his stomach.
He raises a pistol and waves it at me.
Is this it? he asks, and breaks down again.
His laughter is like wheels spinning in gravel.
He can barely talk. I shake my head.
He takes a knife from his belt
and flicks the blade into the sunlight.
This? Again I shake my head. His laughter
has the sound of gears grinding together.
He stamps his feet and takes a small bottle
of mixed pills from the table. This?
he asks. His laughter has the sound of trucks
climbing a steep grade. What could hurt him?
He carries all answers in his pockets.
At last I turn away, shaking my head,
but he neither sees me nor cares as he rolls
back and forth, hooting and kicking his feet
up into the screaming air.

Hunting Ivan Shark

1

I have built an alley for Ivan Shark to walk through.
I spend the morning cleaning knives in preparation.
I bait the alley with my picture, lifelike copies
of my body, clothes still wrapped in my smell. Each
breath he takes is laughter. I keep cleaning my knives.

2

I have dug a pit for Ivan Shark to fall into.
I write his name on all the stakes at the bottom.
I cover them with thin layers of newspaper and place
signs saying this is my constant direction. Each
movement he makes is laughter. I dig more pits.

3

I put stones in high places for Ivan Shark to walk under.
I spend days practicing, dropping them, smashing
pavement, flowers, other stones. I leave my footprints
for him to follow. I even leave my shadow. Each
line in his body is laughter. I keep putting up stones.

Ivan Shark Addresses Me Briefly

You ride fear like a thrown knife.
You are also the target. You watch
your death in the mirror. It
touches you through the glass. Now
it touches you again. You are riding
some animal that is out of control.
You are wearing it down. No matter
where or how you fall, I will be there:
not to catch you but to gather you up.

Part Four

Spider

for C.S.

I am not obvious. I remain
in the corners of your rooms,
riding the silence of eight legs.
I weave my thread to your walls,
protecting you from collapse.
They will not fall.
I take your words, the harsh ones,
and wrap them in silver.
I become their sting,
the bearer of your poison.
Even if you kill me,
I will watch out for you.
See the rain? May it cleanse you.
May you grow with it.
At night when you are sleeping,
my brothers come back to you,
bearing your words of silver between them.
You will be forgiven.

The Television Poems

At first he is asleep and they
    make his life up for him like
    a small house of five rooms
    with a small lawn and small hedge
    and red and yellow flowers.
Perhaps he dreamed; he doesn't remember.

When he wakes, they give him a fordcar.
Then they give him eyes so he can see the road.
They give him a job so he has
    someplace to go.

They give him a name he can easily
    remember. He writes it
    at the tops of pieces of paper.
When he looks out the window,
    they give him a television. Then they
    give him hands so he can work the knobs.
They give him words so he can say:
    Thank you or I am sorry or
    I am content.
When he grows afraid of the silence
    they give him ears. He is
    comforted by the rustling of cloth.

How he earns his living:
All day he bounces a ball
    against a stone wall.
If the ball bounces back to his left,
    he draws a square on his pad.
If it bounces to his right, he draws a circle.
When he catches it, he draws a cross.

They give him clothes and a choice of styles.
They give him a friend who drives a truck.
    Whenever they meet they say:
    I'm fine, are you fine, I'm fine.
They give him emotions so he can like his job.
Pictures of happy children make him happy,
    sad children make him sad.

One day an angel comes down and
    watches him bouncing the ball
    against the stone wall.
His dictionary says it's a bird and he
    gives it half the bun
    from the hamburger that is his lunch.

Who *they* are:
One is the man next door.
When it snows, he shovels his walk.
If it snows all day, he shovels
    his walk five or six times.
At Christmas he gives his wife a perfume called
    I'm Yours. She gives him a tie
    which he wears on their anniversary
    to show he still cares.

They give him money and he buys a brown dog.
    He doesn't know what kind.
The dog likes to chase sticks.
    On Saturdays they go out and he
    throws sticks until his arm hurts.

After a while they give him an election.
   He may choose the man on his left
   or the man on his right.
He is given a small horn to blow.
   It squeaks.
He blows the horn over and over.
He thinks happiness is like that.
He thinks of the sky when
   he drives to work on summer mornings,
   a row of birch at the far edge of a field.

When he is lonely, they give him a wife.
   One year she has blond hair, one year
   it is black.
They give him a loveseat so he can sit
   with his wife. They watch television
   together. They throw sticks for the dog
   together. They go to bed together
   and make love.

One night he dreams of removing his
   wife's breasts and taking them to work.
He tosses them against the wall.
After each toss, he draws a cross.
   They are so perfect.

Who *they* are:
One is the man around the corner.
He has a small mortgage and an eight-
   year-old son who writes letters
   each night to Bobby Orr.
His wife makes fudge brownies and votes.

One year she is secretary of the PTA.
Even in the kitchen she wears her name tag:
Hi, my name is Marge.

When he has worked 50 weeks, he is given
    a two-week vacation.
He and his wife go to the seashore.
All day he sits by the water. He picks up
    stones which he throws in the water. He throws
    sticks and crusts of bread in the water.
One day he sees a white sail far to his left.
For hours he watches it move across the ocean.
    His hands lie in his lap.
When the sail disappears, he goes to sleep.
    He dreams of journeys. He dreams
    of tropical birds with red and yellow feathers,
    cries like sunrise on dark water.
By the time he wakes, he has forgotten the dream.

Who *they* are:
One is the man down the hill.
He has a son who is a boyscout and
    a daughter who wants to be a nurse.
His wife teaches third grade and keeps a
    canary in the classroom. Each weekend
    she lets a different student take it home.
Sometimes they complain about high prices
    but, basically, they believe that life
    is getting better.

Crossroads

*They have married the
ropemaker's daughter and she is
teaching them to fly.* GRIMM

Heights, I never climbed through windows.
Frightened by ladders, I robbed cellars
and the lower floors of houses. I stole shoes,
rugs, guilty secrets. My crimes were quiet.
I'd cut a man's throat only if he were sleeping.
I was too fat to run much. I hated birds
except in honey. Now the wind lives in my hands
and the crows make me thinner each day.
I learn to fly in narrow circles.

Hidden, you knew me by the places
around me, places that I touched
and where now something was missing.
Caught and hung, I became a clown of air.
Secret, I was the hand in your pocket,
the man in your bedroom at night, the reason
your daughter came home crying. Now I'm
a public dancer at the crossroads. Think of me
as you make the small decisions of your life.

Cold, all my choices were warm ones.
No gain could tempt me from the fire.
I robbed the warmest houses, stole the warmest coats.
I worked in summer, burned stores for pleasure;
the blood of your brothers was warm on my hands.
I was hung in August, one of the hottest days,
only to become a signpost of winter.
These are the directions that you too must follow.

The Giver Of Gifts

I am the giver of gifts, the bringer of life.
Everything you are, you are because of me.
You began to move, because I moved behind you.
You began to breathe, because I forced you to run.
I followed you. I tried to take your reflection
from mirrors, your shadow from the face of the earth.
Attempting to escape, you learned touch
through fear of pain. Your own shouts
taught you hearing. I stayed behind you,
giving both warmth and light. Nothing was cold
except around me. There was no darkness
except with me. You received these things
because I taught you. You learned taste and smell
in order to know me. You grew older
in order to put time between us,
unaware that it tied you to me.
Now I give you the final gift. These
wounds are the eyes by which you see me.

The Lives Of The Chosen

The people have lined up for their keys.
They have lined up in buildings of glass
and steel where cleaning women scrub traces
of color from walls and floors. The people
are quiet. They think of golden tomorrows.
They speak only in answer to the names
they have been given. Receiving their keys,
they pay out days of silence, weeks of looking
at nothing. They walk back through empty streets.
The sky is a bandage; each building is a weapon
in a wound. They return to rooms
in apartment houses, rooming houses, exhausted hotels.
They close themselves in. The only sound
is the sound of doors shutting, locks turning.

The people have lined up for their food
in buildings of glass and steel where women
ignorant of English remove traces of color.
The people wait patiently and pay out more days
and weeks. They receive small bags of food
and return to the places where they say they live.
They lock themselves in and eat their food slowly.
They look through magazines of promise and reward.
They find pictures of models with smiles
like wind-swept skies. Cutting out the pictures,
they paste them to their walls. They cover
their walls. The only sound is the sound of breathing.
It could be the sea on empty beaches. The people
stare at the pictures and say they are mirrors.

The people have lined up for their good times
and memories. They have lined up in buildings of glass
and steel where foreign women have removed all color.
The people pay out days on which they may have been
happy, weeks that they don't remember.
They are given small books of memories.
They return to the places where they say they sleep.
Locking their doors, they sit in straight chairs
worth so many days, at tables worth so many weeks.
Occasionally they eat. Constantly they look at
their doors of locks, their walls of many smiles.
They say to themselves: Think of the good times.
The only sound is the sound of pages turning,
like the sound of wind in a forest of dry leaves.

The people line up in buildings without color.
They have eaten their food and now they are tired.
Their faces are the receipts for the years they have given.
Their memories slip from them. Receiving small keys,
they go down to basements and find crates and containers.
Climbing inside, they lock the lids behind them.
The crates are taken to trucks that are waiting.
The people stir and say: Haven't we eaten well.
The trucks leave the city where the sun has gone down.
They drive to fields which the wind crosses like a hand
that will not settle. The trucks are emptied.
Fires are started and the moon rises above them.
The stars wheel above them. The earth rushes
through space like a bullet looking for a target.

The Survival Variation

Trees like apartment buildings, closed
and boarded over. Deerpaths like highways.
Mushrooms, berries, herbs like crowds.
Blades of grass like small individuals.
Walk over them, walk over them—
I survive here. The stones bear
my given names, and everything else likewise.
They are my company and future, my homemade
city, my ruin, my edible population.
The forest keeps my thoughts—a dark
disintegrating green. Looking out
there is no end to it. A home
to be shared with an enemy:
the undoer of the perfectly planned undone.
When I sleep, he changes the paths,
erects new signs. Whatever I call him,
he picks his own names. When I wake
everything shakes with his laughter.

Play In Four Acts

*"I've used a whole bottle of
scent, but my hands still smell. They
smell like the hands of a dead man."*
Captain Solyony in THE THREE SISTERS

I

South was the promise we were born with.
We are waiting to go there. We sit
with our baggage: trunks of summer clothes,
tennis rackets. Our horses lie in their traces;
their legs are broken, have always been broken.
We imagined arriving in that city.
We painted our carriage to look like the sun.
We imagined people running to greet us,
saying how much they had missed us.
Where we live the trains go north.
Our baggage turns white as if touched
by winter: the winter we were leaving,
winter of long delay. The horses shift
in their traces, jangling their bells,
celebrating a departure that has never happened.

2

The way out of the house is not
the door we came through. We imagine it
behind some wall, hidden by rugs,
a door over the roofs to the fields beyond.
We were told where it was. We wrote it down
and lost the paper. The house gets smaller.
We rap on walls for hollow sounds. We stare
from windows facing south, imagining ourselves

beyond the grey hills in a city of color.
There is so little time. We run to each room
searching for a door hidden within us.
We grow smaller. We are like dolls
in a child's toy. The child has followed the sun,
has left us in some attic or far cellar:
the small memory of a forgetful mind.

3
We had pictures of that city, and men came
with stories of its streets and constant laughter.
They brought music and spoke of places
where green is a permanent color.
The men with their pictures are now very old.
Their pictures have yellowed. There are cracks
in streets, buildings where we might have lived.
The edges have turned brown as if burned
by a fire within them. We had our fires.
We gathered around them and talked
of a city where we would go tomorrow,
until tomorrow became another part of winter,
until winter covered our fires, pushed
through our ears and eyes; until our skulls
became its boundaries and we became its creatures.

4
The men with their music have departed,
taking the last colors—pressed flowers,
bits of blue cloth. We try to draw them
from memory—scattered sticks upon a page.

We have said our goodbyes and remained here.
We who are left stand together, gather together
without touching. Our house has walls of ice.
We stand at the windows facing south.
Our world stops at a line of grey hills.
What was beyond them? Our destination surrounds us.
It is the wind we were born to
and have no way to leave. Slowly, we turn
from the windows. The wind turns with us.
We see with the eyes of winter.
We are the ice that has grown within us.

Having My Teeth Cleaned

for Peter Roberts

Nine months since Thanksgiving and now
the turkey makes a small resurrection.
You with clean hands and skin like a fetus,
even the inside of your stomach is rosy.
You draw history from my teeth. Leaping forward,
the turkey hangs in the air as naked as a warning.
My blood rolls off you like rain off a window.
It fills my shoes. It covers the floor. You are
too clean to notice. Even your eyes are white.
Excuse me, white lady, I won't have my teeth cleaned
today or any other. My turkey grows impatient.
I jump from the chair and scoop back the blood
with both my hands. I return old promises,
dinners I was late to, bad poems,
the time I broke Barbara Frame's leg.
You are too clean to see it. I am turning down
your dental floss and three brushings a day.
Whoever called me a difficult baby?
I am returning my dirt to the fold.
Cackling from the window, my turkey waves and leaps.
I run downstairs to save it. Keep your white stories.
What I am, I will always take with me.

Getting Around Town

There is no music in this town.
Twenty-two trumpets strangle eighteen
trombones on 107th Street. The day
is just beginning and I'm losing it already.
People read maps on street corners.
Unsure of their destinations,
they could have come from anywhere.
I read a map on a street corner.
Sidewalk, look at the size of my feet!
People stare into store windows
to see who they are. They wave at themselves.
Who says they aren't friendly?
Joining hands with strangers, I dance
toward the George Washington Bridge.
We have put away unpleasant words.
We wear our best clothes and bright colors.
Reaching our destination, we stop
to admire the view before helping
the sick and elderly over the rail.
Then we follow, toppling into the October sky.
In Palisades Park, a policeman pauses
between arrests. He takes off his cap.
Never before has he been so touched by fall color.

Death Of A Small Businessman

The man in the pet shop is saying
goodbye. All his dogs died yesterday.
Today he's eating his fish. Two feet
from his door and he's up to his knees
in concrete. A slip of the tongue and he's gone.
He tries to save himself. He takes letters
from words scrawled across his windows,
taking a letter from each one, the letters
of his name. He makes his own particular
word of it, not understanding it.
He reads it out loud, not understanding it.
He writes it on the bellies of turtles
and sends them to the sewers.
He writes it on the wings of canaries
and sends them to the sky.
They fly to the park. Already they're homesick.
He writes the word on paper and mails it.
The word travels through sirens which
tear at clouds, bricks which fill the air.
It's delivered to him the next day.
He opens it and reads the word, not
understanding it. His birds
bring the word back to him.
His turtles crawl in through the door.
He reads the word on each one
and turns away, shaking his head.
The man in the pet shop opens his doors.
He shows the word to people on the street.
He points to each letter. He tells of its travels.
They don't understand it. He shows the word
to the mayor who doesn't understand it.
He announces the word on television.

Nobody understands it, although they applaud.
He takes the word and multiplies it
by the years of his life. The answer is zero.
He adds up the people, the moments of waiting,
empty rooms and closed doors. He multiplies it
by the word. The answer is nothing.
At last he writes the word on boards
and builds a coffin. The coffin becomes the word.
He launches the coffin in the river. The river
becomes the word. He floats toward the sun,
sinking into New Jersey. The sun becomes the word.
The coffin sinks into the river.
The man becomes the word.

Seeing Off a Friend

Early April on Broadway, south of Union Square,
a man jumps from a twentieth floor. I
stop him at the tenth. Tell me, I say,
what have you learned in your travels?
We sit and rest awhile. I have only
just asked the question, he says. The answer
will come to me later. He smiles shyly
and continues falling to the fifth floor
where I stop him again. Tell me, I say,
what have you learned in your travels?
He smiles again, being basically cheerful,
but shakes his head. These answers
are slow in approaching, he says,
perhaps it is too soon to tell.
                              Beneath us
the crowd is clamoring for his arrival.
They shout and clap their hands in unison.
They would sing songs of welcome
if they knew them. They would beat drums.
I shrug and let him continue. He falls,
twisting silently. He nicks a streetlight,
smashing it. He hits the hood of a blue
Chevrolet, smashing it. He bounces thirty feet
and hits a parking meter, smashing it.
He lies there as people run toward him.
Their hands are open like shopping bags.
Their mouths are open like pits in the earth.
All his answers cover their faces.

Six Poems On Moving

A SHOUT

I precede you in emergencies. I betray you
in dark places, killing silence. I can be
welcome or warning; dress in fear
or great joy. I have no preference. I exist
only in departure. I leave you breathless.

WHEEL

I was the beginning. Now my children
surround you. You gave them your hands.
Now they have become you. You entrusted me
with your directions, forgetting I was a circle.
Steadily, I carry you toward your finish.

SWORD

Carried, I am your decoration. Swung,
I become you. Born of earth,
drawn from fire, I am blamed for your troubles.
I am guiltless. You alone are the weapon
you are trying to put down.

RAIN

I am nothing when not falling. Touching you,
I am cold. You may run from me.
Touching the earth, I change, changing it.
You may hide. Everything that grows,
grows from my body. You would die without me.

ARROW

I am a song until I stop. Stop me.
You trapped me, dug for me and cut me down.
Now stop me. You gave me to friends, brothers,
even enemies. Now stop me. I return you
to the earth—wrapped in wood, blind to the sky.

CROW

My color is the color of fear. My sound
is of a knife against bone. If I rest,
it is only to watch you. Flying,
I draw darkness behind me like a net.
Now it is over you. Now it is falling.

Part Five

GRIMOIRE

For Susan and Richard

Sloth

If you were running, now you are
walking; if you were walking, now
you are sitting down. I enter
your body as sunlight enters
a forest after a day of rain.
You were on your way to a palm reading,
a new job testing Italian
sports cars, an axe murder. Do it
tomorrow. I am the cat rubbing
against your ankles, the hot bath
after an afternoon of chopping wood.
See me as a feather bed, red and
blue silk cushions in a warm room.
Lie down on me, lie down on me.
Whatever it was, it wasn't important.
Something about someone living or dying or
moving to Phoenix. Something small, no
heavier than the weight which now
presses lightly against your eyelids.
Close them. Tomorrow might be a hard day.

Gluttony

My stomach is the sky
through which the rain falls.

You invite me to your house for dinner;
I restock the shelves of my childhood.

Everything I eat makes me thinner;
I must eat faster.

I send myself love notes
and swell like a flower.

Everyone around me looks small and
insubstantial, like men adrift in a lifeboat.
I am the island they see in the distance.

Boredom

Wednesday evening, rain on the streets;
Chinese waiter at a table by the window,
soiled white apron—the restaurant is empty.
He is looking at a magazine about Taiwan;
elbows on the table, chin in his hands:
girls in silk dresses offer bouquets of
red flowers under an impossible sky.

Crow sits on my heart. It
will not sleep, will not
leave; it will not sing.
I try to name it: Claw-
foot, Blackwing. It draws
my words from me, takes my breath.

Play solitaire with 50 cards.
Do Bogart impersonations in your mirror.
Ask someone to explain the Wankel engine.
After writing your life story, read it.

Anger

I am the simplest of disguises.
Putting me on, you fling yourself
at your victim. Taking me off,
you are the chance witness, finding
the weapon, just happening by.

The animal within him is hungry.

His hands come in boxes.
His skin is lined with knives.
His head is a mixture of phosphorus and
sulphur: strike him anywhere.

Despair

I become your wardrobe;
you wear me like a sack of stones.

I become your books;
everywhere you read of your death.

I become your friends;
we go off without you.

I become your house;
it falls down around you.

I become your lover;
you would rather sleep alone.

Hunger

Three men throw sticks
at a scarecrow
in a dusty field:
dry as the eyes
at a rich man's
funeral, flat
as an empty plate.

_____

Coffin standing on end,
lined with shelves.
Open the lid,
a light goes on.

_____

When you leave, I lick the sheets.

Fear

New Year's Day, at the end of the farm lane
where it meets another, where three roads meet,
we find a block of wood in the old snow.
Three hatchet marks are cut into one end,
and blood, blood also on the snow. A dozen
white feathers are scattered around it.
We find no car tracks or clear footprints leading
to or from the county road half a mile away.
None of our neighbors raise chickens and there are
no trees for several hundred yards. The three roads
lead only to this part of the field where someone
chose to bring a chicken, hatchet and block of wood
to hold some ceremony this New Year's Day.

———————————

Don't stare too long at your shadow
in case you see it move without you.
Don't look at the trap door to the attic
in case you see it beginning to open.
Don't let your hand hang over the bed
in case something takes it while you sleep.

———————————

You find me at the back of your closet:
rags and hogbristles, wax and straw,
small puppet with a white china head,
body stuck with pins, smeared with blood.
A black cloth covers my eyes.
You recognize my fingernails and hair
which are yours. You recognize my clothes

cut from your own black suit.
You read your name on the tag around my neck.
You forget what you were looking for when you
reached into this corner and touched me.

Dignity

Something to stand on: stone
to raise me above your heads.
Who could doubt my vision?

Something to wrap myself in:
monkey-skin to keep me warm.
Who could be better dressed?

Something to lie down in: deep
hole to pull around me, final argument.
Who could contradict me?

Covetousness

Keep your toys and small possessions;
I only want your hands.
Everything I touch feels like it's mine.

———————————

He does his shopping in the houses of his friends.

———————————

I dreamt I was you, sleeping with your wife,
dreaming you were me, sleeping with mine.

Greed

I come to your house and paint it grey;
I come into your room and make it smaller:
your television is smaller, the bed squeaks.
The man next door has a nicer fedora.
Were you happy? Were you content?
Your dog needs a rhinestone collar.

———————————

You flatter yourself with presents;
it's the thought that counts—
golf shoes, wedding rings—
like a tree holding sunlight,
a sieve holding water.

———————————

He was born with small hands, deep pockets.

Dancing

On my feet, grain ships
out of the Black Sea.
Dancing: storm warnings
circle the Mediterranean.
You from Pompeii,
do you remember the other party?

Treads of a tank
when I'm walking. Coffins
when I'm sitting down.
Now there is music.
Here is something the birds carry.

Looking out from mountaintop
and warpaint, you see the cavalry
galloping through the valley. You run
shouting for your friends.
Not only am I dancing, I am singing.

Spite

I steal your mailbox, leave
gum on your sidewalk. I
seduce your sister, ignore your wife.
I tear one page from each of your books.
I convince you that I am your friend.

_____

When people ask about you,
I shake my head. When they
tell about you, I nod.

_____

Today, I hang myself
from a greased flagpole
outside your picture window.
Yesterday, I stole your curtains.

Bravado

for P.G.

Smart, stupid—let me tell you how to do it.
I could teach the rose about blooming, the
porpoise about swimming. I could write a book.
I could tell the dictionary about words.
Tight-rope walking? Bring me a ball of string.
Juggling? Just give me a dozen eggs.
If you never ask, you'll never know.
Wherever I go, doors open like women,
women open like baby birds, men shut up
like clams out of water. I teach popes
about praying, generals about fighting.
Music? I whistle operas. Painting?
Let me draw on your wall. Poems?
I've just shown you how to write one.

Envy

You invite me to a banquet in your honor;
I bring my own dinner: ash and vinegar.

You won a prize
where I wasn't a judge.

I put on the news of your success
like a coat of nails.
Each step I take
is another reason to hate you.

Absence

If these lines that I
see appearing on my face
were the lines of a map,
I would be with you now.

If the distance between us
were as tangible as the ice
that I feel, you would see me
sliding toward you, full of
joy at having found you, sorrow
at having been gone so long.

If my memory had the body
of a servant or thief
I would pursue it until it
returned what it had stolen:
already it blurs your face
with the faces of strangers.

Vanity

He lines the walls with mirrors,
floor and ceiling with mirrors.
He claps and blows kisses to the crowd.

―――――――――

I write this,
you read this.

―――――――――

His life story reads like a cookbook.
His telephone has two mouthpieces, no receiver.
He wears fur coats inside out.

Patience

You are born to parents who love you.
They give you a gold spoon or they don't. They
may be Spanish or Norwegian. I am waiting.

You go to school to learn numbers. You
master geometry or don't. Your friends
either mock or respect you. I am waiting.

You either marry or travel to Baghdad. You
have children who love you or don't. You work
for yourself or the railroad. I am waiting.

You dream of apples and the Portuguese
maid. You either embezzle or don't. Your hair
turns grey, heart greyer. I am waiting.

You regret that you gave up smoking. You
receive a gold watch or you don't. The only
door left is the last one; I am waiting.

Doubt

I listen carefully but hear only lies.
My clothes feel like someone else's.
My wife tells me nothing I want to know.
My mirror tells the story in which I am villain.

Cars break down. Better walk.
Might slip. Better walk slowly.
Might meet a mugger. Better
stay home. TV might break.
Better sit quietly. Air
full of teeth. Don't breathe.
Better sleep. Bad dreams.

He sees his past as the road to a house;
he is afraid to open the door.
He sees his present as a foreign city;
he left his map at the hotel.
He sees his future as deepening water;
he has forgotten how to swim.

Grief

Trying to remember you
is like carrying water
in my hands a long distance
across sand. Somewhere
people are waiting.
They have drunk nothing for days.

Your name was the food I lived on;
now my mouth is full of dirt and ash.
To say your name was to be surrounded
by feathers and silk; now, reaching out,
I touch glass and barbed wire.
Your name was the thread connecting my life;
now I am fragments on a tailor's floor.

I was dancing when I
learned of your death; may
my feet be severed from my body.

Silence

I am the music you were born to.
Then you put me aside, wanting your own;
like sticks scratching together, you wanted your own.
I am the song you will sing longest.

I am the clothing you were born in.
Then you changed me for bright reds and blues;
like a clown or bridegroom you wanted everything perfect.
Death is a marriage; you will wear me to the wedding.

I am the house you were born in.
Then you left me and went traveling;
like a child without parents or fortune you went traveling.
I am where you are going.

Stephen Dobyns

Stephen Dobyns was born in Orange, New
Jersey, in 1941, and raised in New Jersey,
Michigan, Virginia and Pennsylvania. He was
educated at Shimer College, Wayne State
University and the University of Iowa. His jobs
have included teaching at various colleges and
working as a reporter for the Detroit *News*. His
book of poems, *Concurring Beasts*, was the
Lamont Poetry Selection for 1971.
He has written two novels:
A Man of Little Evils (1973) and
Saratoga Longshot (1976).
He currently lives in Cambridge, Massachusetts.